DO-4U THE ROBOT

EXPERIENCES

FORCES AND MOTION

Worldwide Robotics

by
Mark Weakland

illustrated by
Mike Moran

PICTURE WINDOW BOOKS
a capstone imprint

Thanks to our advisers for their expertise, research, and advice:
Dr. Paul Ohmann, Associate Professor of Physics, University of St. Thomas
Terry Flaherty, PhD, Professor of English, Minnesota State University, Mankato

Editor: **Shelly Lyons**
Designer: **Lori Bye**
Art Director: **Nathan Gassman**
Production Specialist: **Danielle Ceminsky**
The illustrations in this book were created digitally.

Picture Window Books
1710 Roe Crest Drive
North Mankato, MN 56003
www.capstonepub.com

Library of Congress Cataloging-in-Publication Data
Weakland, Mark.
Do-4U the robot experiences forces and motion / by Mark Weakland ;
illustrated by Mike Moran.
p. cm. — (In the science lab)
Includes index.
ISBN 978-1-4048-7145-8 (library binding)
ISBN 978-1-4048-7239-4 (paperback)
1. Robots—Juvenile literature. 2. Robots—Motion—Juvenile
literature. 3. Force and energy—Juvenile literature. I. Moran,
Michael, 1957- ill. II. Title. III. Title: Do for you the robot
experiences forces and motion.
TJ211.2.W43 2012
629.8'92—dc23
2011025846

Printed in the United States of America in North Mankato, Minnesota.
042019   001869

WELCOME TO WORLDWIDE ROBOTICS!

I'm D4, a helper bot. You can call me DO-4U. That's because I do work for you. My partner is a HV1 model. But everyone calls him HEV-E1.

Workers at Worldwide Robotics build robots. To build a bot, they need to know how and why objects move. In other words, they have to be experts on force and motion.

Come into the lab and see our robots using force and motion. They're doing work, so you don't have to!

TO DO WORK, A ROBOT MUST MOVE. IN HIS RESTING POSITION, HEV-E1 IS DOING NEITHER! THE FORCE OF GRAVITY IS PULLING ON HIM. IT HELPS HEV-E1 STAY AT REST. HOW WILL I GET HIM UP AND MOVING?

An object won't move unless a force acts upon it.
Most forces can be thought of as a push or pull.
It's force that sets everything, including HEV-E1, into motion.

AN OBJECT'S TENDENCY TO STAY AT REST IS CALLED INERTIA. HEV-E1 HAS A LOT OF IT BECAUSE HE IS BIG AND HEAVY. TO MOVE HIM TO A NEW POSITION, I'VE ... GOT ... TO USE ... A LOT ... OF FORCE. OOF! COME ON, BIG GUY, TIME TO POWER UP!

A huge robot like HEV-E1 is great at guarding your bedroom. Pesky brothers and sisters simply aren't strong enough to move him.

LARGE FORCES ARE NEEDED TO MOVE OBJECTS WITH LARGE AMOUNTS OF INERTIA. OTHER OBJECTS, SUCH AS THESE CRUMBS AND THIS DUST, HAVE VERY LITTLE INERTIA. EVEN A SMALL FORCE, LIKE MY BRUSH, WILL GET THEM MOVING.

Ah-choo!

While HEV-E1 guards, I clean. Cleaning is all about using force to get something done. First, electric motors apply force to move my arm. Next, my arm applies force to the dirty underwear.

PWING!

WWR

a lever in action

SIMPLE MACHINES, SUCH AS LEVERS, LET US DO MORE WITH LESS FORCE. MY ARM AND ELBOW WORK AS A LEVER. WITH A LEVER I CAN FLING UNDERWEAR FAR.

ALL WORK AND NO PLAY MAKES FOR A BORING BOT. HERE AT THE TESTING GROUNDS, ROBOTS TEST OBJECTS IN MOTION AND HAVE SOME FUN!

10

Every robot in motion used a push or pull to get moving. The robots will continue to swing, spin, and roll until another force acts upon them. This is true of all objects.

ONLY ANOTHER FORCE CAN MAKE A MOVING OBJECT CHANGE ITS COURSE OR STOP.

When a robot rolls down a hill, it picks up speed. Speed describes how fast an object is moving. Acceleration describes how much speed the object is picking up.

Gravity is the force that pulls all objects toward the center of Earth. It's pulling on HEV-E1 right now—that's why he's accelerating.

THE RU-33 ROBOT IS ACCELERATING EVEN FASTER THAN HEV-E1. WHY? THE FORCE OF GRAVITY IS PULLING AND THE FORCE OF THE JET PACK IS PUSHING. IN THIS CASE, TWO FORCES ARE BETTER THAN ONE. GOOD THING THAT ROBOT'S WEARING A HELMET!

friction

friction

Not all forces work to get something moving. Friction works against motion. When two objects slide past each other, their rough parts rub. This rubbing is known as friction. Friction works on skateboard wheels and swing set chains.

When there's little friction, moving objects come to rest slowly. When friction is great, moving objects slow down quickly. Dragging a skateboard's tail will slow it down fast. There's a lot of friction between the skateboard and the pavement.

This tail is smokin'!

friction

IF THERE'S ENOUGH FRICTION, THE SKATEBOARD WILL STOP IMMEDIATELY.

Summer is a great time for bare feet. But watch out—you don't want to step on a nail or rusty piece of metal! Don't worry. With my arm attachments, I will use magnetism to clean your yard. My magnets pull iron or steel objects to them.

LIKE FRICTION AND GRAVITY, MAGNETISM IS A TYPE OF FORCE.

Objects are usually moved with an actual push or pull. But magnets push and pull objects without touching them. That's because magnets use a magnetic field. It surrounds the magnet like an invisible bubble. The magnetic field causes the force that pulls iron or steel to the magnet.

magnetic field

MAGNETISM AND GRAVITY ARE FORCES THAT WORK THROUGH SOLIDS, LIQUIDS, AND GASES. MY MAGNETIC ARM PULLS METAL THROUGH THE AIR. THE MAGNET WILL ALSO WORK THROUGH PAPER, PLASTIC, AND WOOD.

MAGNETISM AND GRAVITY ARE FORCES THAT FADE ACROSS DISTANCE. A MAGNET'S PULL ON METAL WEAKENS AS THE MAGNET AND METAL MOVE APART.

GRAVITY IS SIMILAR. IF AN OBJECT IS NEAR THE GROUND, GRAVITY'S PULL IS STRONG. IF THE OBJECT IS HIGH IN THE AIR, GRAVITY'S PULL WEAKENS.

DO-4U, the force is with you!

GRAVITY
MISSION
SUCCESSFUL!

Worldwide
Robotics

21

Thanks for visiting Worldwide Robotics. You've learned a lot about forces and motion during your visit. Now put your knowledge to work. Move an object with a magnet. Figure out the best way to lift a heavy object. Or build a robot that flings your dirty underwear!

REMEMBER, ROBOTS DO YOUR WORK SO YOU DON'T HAVE TO!

PWING!

GLOSSARY

acceleration—the change in speed of a moving object

force—any action that changes the movement of an object

friction—a force produced when two objects rub against each other; friction slows down objects

gravity—a force that pulls objects together; gravity pulls objects toward the center of Earth

inertia—the tendency of an object to remain either at rest or in motion unless a force acts upon it

lever—a bar that turns on a resting point and is used to lift items

magnetic field—an area around a magnet that affects other objects

magnetism—the natural force of a magnet, which pulls it to iron or steel

TO LEARN MORE

More Books to Read

Conrad, David. *Gravity All Around*. Physical Science. Mankato, Minn.: Capstone Press, 2011.

Royston, Angela. *Forces and Motion*. My World of Science. Chicago: Heinemann Library, 2008.

Weakland, Mark. *Zombies and Forces and Motion*. Monster Science. Mankato, Minn.: Capstone Press, 2012.

Internet Sites

FactHound offers a safe, fun way to find Internet sites related to this book. All of the sites on FactHound have been researched by our staff.

Here's all you do:

Visit *www.facthound.com*

Type in this code: 9781404871458

Super-cool stuff! Check out projects, games and lots more at www.capstonekids.com

INDEX

LOOK FOR ALL THE BOOKS IN THE SERIES:

CAPTAIN KIDD'S CREW
EXPERIMENTS WITH
SINKING AND FLOATING

DO-4U THE ROBOT
EXPERIENCES
FORCES AND MOTION

GERTRUDE and REGINALD the Monsters
Talk about
LIVING AND NONLIVING

JOE-JOE THE WIZARD BREWS UP
SOLIDS, LIQUIDS, AND GASES